Psychology and Health Series:
Volume 1

STRESS

WE CAN MASTER IT

Marios Savva

I dedicate all my books in my Psychology and Health series, to my loving family.

TABLE OF CONTENTS

Introduction: The Definition of Stress _____ 1
Stress Explained _____ 4
Changing Our Thoughts _____ 7
What is Anxiety? _____ 9
Managing and Coping _____ 12
Managing and Coping II_____ 15
Managing and Coping III _____ 18
Moderating Our Stress _____ 21
Buffering Our Stress_____ 23
Anxiety and Worrying _____ 25
Anxiety Disorders_____ 28
Anxiety Disorders II _____ 30
Panic Attacks _____ 32
Post Traumatic Stress _____ 35

THE AUTHOR

As an experienced psychologist currently living in Birmingham, England, and a member of the British Psychological Society, I now have the fervent desire to start writing books on psychology for people to read. I have endeavoured to make my books interesting to read and, with a little humour, as some psychology material can get 'heavy' and slightly complicated. STRESS: WE CAN MASTER IT, is the first book in the Psychology and Health series. Readers can contact me on: marios.spurs@hotmail.co.uk.

Other books by the author

Depression and Sadness

Body Image

Know Thyself

Drugs and Addictions

I Want To Sleep

Introduction: The Definition of Stress

Stress is terrible. In fact, in this day and age it has become the bane of our existence. In fact, scientists have projected that in approximately twenty years it will overtake AIDS as the number one cause of deaths worldwide. That's how terrible it is.

Stress causes great harm and affects us not only psychologically but also physiologically as well; flushed cheeks, irritable stomach, bloated intestines, tensed and aching muscles, migraines, to mention a few, are often tell-tale signs of stress. Stress for each of us can come and go, but prolonged stress levels can have even more serious effects on our health leading to heart disease, serious digestive disorders, and can even raise cholesterol levels.

So, what exactly is stress? Stress is defined as the process by which we perceive and respond to certain events called 'stressors'[1] that we appraise as challenging or threatening. It is an event that exerts physical or psychological force or pressure on a person, and the demand made on a person to adapt, cope, or adjust.

Some stress is healthful and necessary to keep us alert and occupied. This has been called by some researchers as **'eustress'**. But intense or prolonged stress can overtax our adjustment capacity, affect our moods, impair our ability to experience pleasure, and harm the body, as mentioned above.

There are many sources of stress: daily hassles, life changes, pain and discomfort, conflict, irrational beliefs, Type A[2] behaviour, and environmental factors like disasters, noise, and crowding. Stress arises less from events themselves than from how we appraise them. One person may regard an event as a welcoming challenge; another appraises it as risking failure.

When perceived as challenges, stressors can have positive effects, arousing and motivating people to conquer the difficulties they face, to be successful in performing a certain task well. Successful

1

athletes thrive and excel when aroused by a challenge. As already mentioned, stress depends on how individuals cognitively appraise and interpret events; it is how individuals personally perceive and interpret the various events in their lives as harmful, threatening, or challenging AND their determination of whether they have the resources to effectively cope with such events. Conflict, frustration, and overload can also lead to stress; stimuli may become so intense/prolonged that we may not be able to cope.

Personality differences influence the extent to which we are affected by stress and the ways in which we cope with it. People with different personalities respond to life stresses in different ways. People who are easygoing or psychologically hardy[3] are more resilient under the impact of stress. Psychologically hardy people have a strong sense of control. A sense of loss of control can heighten stress and impair the immune system. It might surprise you to learn that DNA[4] is frequently damaged but that it has the capacity to repair itself. Research shows that defective DNA repair capacity is involved in the development of cancer, and that DNA works hardest to repair itself during times of stress.

Emotions motivate certain kinds of behaviour. Negative emotions such as anxiety, anger, and depression can motivate us to behave in maladaptive ways. For example, anxiety tends to motivate escape behaviour; anger motivates aggressive behaviour; and depression motivates withdrawal. It is helpful for us to perceive negative emotional responses as signs that something is wrong, to learn what we can about the sources of our stress, and then to plan behaviour that will enable us to remove or buffer stressors. But when our emotions run too high, they can disrupt our cognitive processes and interfere with our adaptive behaviour. Under stress we may have difficulty thinking clearly or remaining focused on the task at hand.

The stress impact of an event reflects the meaning of the event to a person. Pregnancy, for example, can be a positive or negative life change, depending on whether one wants, and is prepared to have a child. We appraise stressful events in terms of their perceived danger, our values and goals, our beliefs in our coping ability, and our social support.

You may read about the role of irrational beliefs in stress in the other chapters in this book.

[1] Stressors are events or challenges or threats that we appraise as threatening or challenging. In this context, stressors can threaten our resources- our job security, our loved one's health or well-being, our deeply held beliefs, our self-image.

[2] TYPE A personality is someone who is excessively competitive, hard-driven, impatient, perfectionist, hostile, aggressive, unwilling to relinquish control, and has a sense of time urgency. Additionally, it is the type of personality that research has shown to be related to heart disease.

[3] Psychologically hardy individuals are more resilient to the effects of stress. They are committed to their work and other activities, are open to new challenges, and feel in control of their lives.

[4] DNA (deoxyribonucleic acid) is a complex molecule containing genetic information that makes up the chromosomes.

Stress Explained

Our beliefs about events, as well as the events themselves can be stressors that challenge our ability to adjust. For example, beliefs such as "there's nothing I can do about it" or "I am a no good failure", are exaggerations which compound misery, foster helplessness, internalize blame and divert us from planning and deciding what to do next.

Anxieties about the future and depression over a loss are normal and to be expected. However some of our beliefs tend to catastrophize things that happen to us, which subsequently, contributes to anxiety or depression. When an individual's emotional reaction heightens, let's say in the case of a loss, so do feelings of helplessness; these types of beliefs impair coping ability and lower a person's expectations that they can master problems and produce positive outcomes.

Many of us adopt irrational beliefs that become our personal doorways to unhappiness and stress. We may make ourselves miserable by adopting different kinds of irrational beliefs such as:

* You must have the sincere love of everyone and approval of almost everyone who is important to you almost all the time.

* You must succeed in virtually everything you attempt in order to feel that you are a competent person.

* Things must go the way you want them to go or life is just awful.

* When there is danger or fear in your world, you must be preoccupied with it and be continually upset by it.

* Your emotional misery stems from external pressures that you have little or no ability to control. Unless these external pressures change, you must remain miserable.

* It is easier to evade life's responsibilities and problems than to face them and undertake new challenges.

When we hold to these kinds of beliefs, we inevitably find that either we or the world at large comes up short, which leaves us feeling upset, angry, or depressed. It is understandable that we would want the approval of others, but it is irrational to believe that we cannot survive without it. It would be nice to be competent in everything we do, but it is unreasonable to expect it.

Although childhood experiences can explain the origins of irrational beliefs, it is our own cognitive appraisal -here and now- that causes us to be miserable.

Research findings support the connections between irrational beliefs (e.g. excessive dependence on social approval and perfectionism) and feelings of anxiety and depression. Indeed, perfectionists are more likely to commit suicide when they are depressed.

Our thoughts and behaviour influence each other. We can be our own worst enemies when stressors strike. For example do these experiences sound familiar?

1. You want to express your genuine feelings but think that you might upset another person by doing so?

2. You haven't been able to get to sleep for 15 minutes and assume that you will lie awake the whole night and feel 'wrecked' in the morning?

3. You're not sure what decision to make, so you try to put your conflicts out of your mind by going out, playing cards or watching TV?

4. You decide not to play tennis or go jogging because your form isn't perfect and you're in less than perfect condition?

If you have had such experiences, it may be because you harbour some sort of irrational beliefs - beliefs that make you overly concerned about the approval of others (2) or perfectionist (5). They may lead you to think you can relieve yourself of life's problems by pretending they do not exist (4), or that a minor setback <u>must</u> lead to greater problems (1 & 3). The unjustified assumption that an event is or will become awful is called catastrophizing. That is, you turn a setback into a catastrophe.

What can we do to change this tide? You may see ways in the upcoming chapters.

Changing Our Thoughts

In the previous chapter we saw how the thinking patterns we have may either undermine us against stressors, and thus feel their impact more intensely, or, buffer us against them and thus mediate the resulting impact.

How, then, do we change irrational or catastrophizing thoughts? There is a challengingly simple answer: We change these thoughts by changing them. However, change can require some work. Before we can change our thoughts we must first be, or become, aware of them. You may now look at the ensuing multi-step procedure for controlling the irrational or catastrophizing thoughts that often accompany feelings of anxiety, conflict, or tension.

First, develop awareness of the thoughts that seem to be making you miserable by careful self-examination. Look at the examples of irrational beliefs at the beginning of this book and ask yourself whether any of them rings true of you. Also: When you encounter anxiety or frustration, pay close attention to your thoughts.

Second, evaluate the accuracy of the thoughts. Are they guiding you toward a solution or are they compounding your problems? Do they reflect reality or do they blow things out of proportion? Do they misplace the blame for failure or shortcomings? And so on.

Then, prepare thoughts that are <u>incompatible</u> with the irrational or catastrophizing thoughts and then practice saying them firmly to yourself. (If nobody is nearby, why not say them firmly aloud? saying thoughts aloud aids rationalizing.)

Finally, reward yourself with a mental pat on the back for making effective changes in your beliefs and thought patterns.

Controlling catastrophizing thoughts reduces the impact of a stressor, whether it is pain, anxiety, or feelings of frustration. It gives you a chance to develop a plan for effective action. When effective action is not possible, controlling our thoughts increases our capacity to tolerate discomfort. So does relaxing, or at least trying to relax.

What is Anxiety?

Anxiety - the distress evoked by life's pressures - is a negative mood state characterized by marked negative affect and bodily symptoms of physical tension in which a person apprehensively anticipates future danger or misfortune.

When anxiety helps us prepare to deal with some danger then it has served us well. But in modern life, anxiety is more often out of proportion and out of place. Distress comes in the face of situations that we must live with or that are conjured by the mind, not real dangers we need to confront. Repeated bouts of anxiety signal high levels of stress.

Most of us feel anxiety almost every day of our lives. Even thinking about things might make you nervous. Surprisingly though, in moderate amounts, anxiety is good for us. Psychologists have known for nearly a century that we perform better when we are a little anxious. You would not have done so well on that test if you had had no anxiety. You were a little more charming and lively on that date last weekend because you were anxious. And you will be better prepared for that job interview coming up if you are anxious. In short, physical and intellectual performances are driven and enhanced by anxiety. Without it, very few of us would get much done.

One psychologist called anxiety the "shadow of intelligence." He thought the human ability to plan in some detail for the future was connected to that gnawing feeling that things could go wrong and we had better be prepared for them. This is why anxiety is a future-oriented mood state. If you were to put it into words you might say, "Something might go wrong, and I'm not sure I can deal with it, but I've got to be ready to try." "Maybe I'd better study a little harder (or check the mirror one more time before my date, or do a little more research on that company before the interview")."

But what happens when you have too much anxiety? You might

9

actually fail the exam because you can't concentrate on the questions. All you can think about when you're too anxious is how terrible it will be if you fail. You might blow the interview for the same reason. On that date with a new person, you might spend the evening with perspiration running off your face, a sick feeling in your stomach, unable to think of one interesting thing to say. Too much of a good thing can be harmful, and very few sensations are more harmful than anxiety that is out of control.

What makes the situation worse is that severe anxiety usually doesn't go away, that is, even if we "know" there is really nothing to be afraid of, we remain anxious. We constantly see examples of this kind of irrationality. Individuals, who suffer from anxiety-based disorders such as claustrophobia, are well aware that there is little to fear in the situations they find so stressful. As is the case with irrational beliefs, some people feel the need to focus on things that distress them. They may be unwilling to allow themselves to be distracted from pain and discomfort.

In looking at the psychological contributions for anxiety, we can say that they originated from the study of unconscious behaviours. Freud viewed anxiety as a psychic reaction to danger surrounding the reactivation of an infantile fear situation. A contemporary, more integrated approach, postulates that youngsters initially obtain a perception that events are not always under their control and that this is dangerous. This sense of control emerges through interaction with parents that are encouraging, predictable and responsive to a child's needs, whereas a sense of uncontrollability seems related to parents that fail to provide a secure home and parents that are often overprotective and over-intrusive. Such a perception of uncontrollability is a central psychological risk factor that increases a person's vulnerability to anxiety later in life.

We may therefore conclude that a child who has no sense of control and predictability may most likely develop a predisposition[1] for anxiety in later life. Thus, familial influences seem to have a strong influence in the development of anxiety disorders.

People are more sensitive to anxiety than others; this has a lot to do with our genetic make-up. One maybe born with a biological vulnerability[2] to be anxious. But for this diathesis for anxiety to be activated, then this biological vulnerability must also interact with socialized beliefs that events are uncontrollable as well as having the experience of life stressors and learning experiences.

The level of anxiety one has when facing an event/situation depends, among other things, on their predisposition (biological vulnerability) to anxiety. A person who has high trait-anxiety[3] will perceive many situations as anxiety-provoking and will have to engage in more relaxation techniques and self-talk than a person who does not have high trait-anxiety.

[1&2] The terms predisposition and biological vulnerability refer to the same construct. They refer to those characteristics and elements of our personality which have been inherited through our genetic make-up from family members.

[3] The term trait-anxiety is the natural anxiety threshold of an individual which stems from his traits. Traits are people's characteristic patterns of behaviour and conscious motives or a disposition to feel and act.

Managing and Coping

Unfortunately, stress is inevitable in our everyday lives. As we have seen, it can harm us in different ways. But, there are ways to manage stress and buffer its impact on us.

Stress management is a set of techniques designed to help us manage the stress we experience more effectively- to prevent stress from becoming a source of distress. Some people have good coping resources for handling stress. But others rely on defensive means of coping with it. Do you choose defensive coping or active coping?

Many techniques for coping with stress are defensive. Defensive coping reduces the immediate impact of the stressor, but at a cost. Costs include socially inappropriate behaviour (as in alcoholism, aggression, or regression), avoidance of problems (as in withdrawal), or self-deception (as in rationalization[1] or denial).

Defensive coping grants us time to marshal our resources but does not deal with the source of stress or enhance the effectiveness of our responses to stress. In the long run, defensive methods can be harmful if we do not use the chance they provide to find better ways of coping. There are several ways of defensive coping:

Withdrawal: When you face a stressful situation you feel unable to control, you may wish to withdraw from the situation. Withdrawal can be emotional, as in loss of interest, or physical, as in moving or changing one's lifestyle. Temporary withdrawal can be helpful by providing the chance to find better methods of coping. But withdrawal from social involvement prevents people from getting on with their lives and finding other sources of support.

Denial: People who rely on denial when facing the stress of coping with a serious illness refuse to acknowledge the seriousness of their health situation. They may minimize the seriousness of their condition ("Oh, it's no big deal."), erroneously attribute their symptoms to benign causes ("It's probably just my arthritis acting up"), or assume that symptoms will pass if left alone. Denial may minimize the effects of stress in the short run, but the eventual consequences of leaving serious problems such as medical ones untreated can be tragic. Sigmund Freud, acknowledged as the 'father' of psychoanalysis, considered denial a type of defence mechanism that operates unconsciously to protect us from anxiety that might stem from recognition of unacceptable ideas and impulses. According to this psychodynamic theory[2], everyone uses defence mechanisms, at least to some degree. Defence mechanisms become problems when people begin to rely on them to cope with stress, or when they lead people to forgo necessary medical treatment or make other desirable life changes.

Substance Use: Another common, but also ineffective, means of handling stressful situations is the use of alcohol or other drugs. The use of psychoactive substances may blunt awareness of the sources of stress, but fails to resolve the underlying problem. Moreover, drinking regularly or using other drugs to cope with stress can lead to a drug dependence, which only compounds the problems the person is facing.

Aggression: Some people lose their tempers when they feel stressed and become verbally or physically abusive to other people. Violence is often used to cope with social provocations and, sometimes, as a response to frustration. But lashing out at others verbally or physically is a source of stress in itself, can damage relationships, and can have serious consequences, even lethal consequences in the case of physical assault. Physical violence is not only illegal, but is also dangerous. Aggressive behaviour also heightens interpersonal conflict by creating motives for retaliation.

As mentioned above, methods of defensive coping with stress-such as drinking, withdrawal, of defensive mechanisms can reduce the immediate impact of the stressor, but with some cost. Costs include socially inappropriate behaviour (as in drinking heavily), avoidance of problems (as in withdrawal), or self deception (as in

13

the use of some defence mechanisms). The ways of dealing with stress mentioned in this chapter come under the term called **Defensive Coping**. But there are far better ways to deal with stress, and these come under the term called *Active Coping*. You may read about this in the chapter Managing and Coping (II).

[1] Rationalization is a defence mechanism, according to the psychoanalysis theory, that involves reinterpreting our behaviour to make it seem more rational and acceptable to us. We excuse or justify a threatening thought or action (that induces anxiety in us) by persuading ourselves there is a rational explanation for it.

[2] Psychodynamic theory, also called psychoanalytic theory, is based on Sigmund Freud's theory of personality and system of therapy for treating mental disorders. His theory was a quest to understand the conflict between human passion and reason. It was Freud's lifework to explore the complex ways that irrationality clashes against rationality. His main focus was on the workings on the unconscious and how it influences us.

Managing and Coping II

In the previous chapter we focused on Defensive Coping in handling stress. We shall now see healthier ways to manage to stress which come under the term called Active Coping.

As we saw in Defensive ways of coping, some ways of handling stress can make matters much worse. Direct or active coping methods for managing stress aim to manipulate the environment[1] (in socially acceptable ways) to remove stressors, or to change our response patterns to buffer their harmfulness. Through active coping, we willingly face stressors for what they are. Sometimes they cannot be eliminated or modified. Active coping then involves rational evaluation of our capacities to manage them as best we can and planning efficient ways to cushion their impact.

The following are strategies for active coping with the stressors of everyday life:

Keep Stress at Manageable levels

*Don't bite off more than you can chew. Don't take on more tasks than you can reasonably accomplish given the other demands on your time. Be careful not to sacrifice all your personal needs.

*Reduce daily hassles. What can you do to reduce daily hassles? For example, might you be able to change your schedule to avoid the morning traffic jam? What other daily hassles can you minimize or eliminate?

*Develop time-management skills. Sometimes it may seem like there's never enough time to accomplish all that you need to do. There is much you can do to make time work for you rather than against you. For example, prioritize things you need to do, break down larger tasks into smaller ones, take things more slowly.

Become More Aware of Your Body's Response to Stress

Don't ignore the signs of stress. Become aware of how your body reacts to stress. Does your back hurt more than usual? Is that nagging headache becoming a daily occurrence? Are you biting your nails? Are you exhausted at the end of the day? These physical and psychological symptoms may signal that you've reached or exceeded your stress threshold. Also, prepare your body for coping with stress. Follow a nutritionally balanced diet. Get enough sleep. Have regular medical check-ups. Avoid tobacco and other harmful substances. Keep active and fit.

Know What to Expect

Stressors are more manageable when you know what to expect. Knowing what to expect gives you time to develop coping strategies. For example, people with accurate knowledge of medical procedures tend to cope with them more effectively than people who remain in the dark. When you face a particular stressor, learn what you can about it.

Reach Out and Be Touched by Someone

Social support buffers the effects of stress. Studies with medical students and dental students, two highly stressed groups, show that students who had more friends had better immune system functioning than those with fewer friends. Indeed, lonely people have poorer immune system functioning than people with more social support. Hospitalized people who receive strong emotional support have speedier recoveries than people with weak emotional-support networks. Receiving social support is only one side of the proverbial coin. Giving support to others can also help buffer the impact of your stress and can be personally fulfilling. Look at how you can broaden your own social support network so that you may get the kind of social support that you can rely upon, especially in times of stress.

To see the rest of the strategies for active coping with the stressors of everyday life, look at the next chapter- Managing and Coping (III).

[1] The term environment in this context does not mean the natural environment around us as such, i.e. sky, trees, buildings etc. In psychology, the term environment refers to every non-genetic influence, from prenatal (the period before giving birth) to the people and things around us.

Managing and Coping III

In continuation from the previous chapter on active coping strategies for dealing with everyday stressors, here are some others:

Work It Out by Working Out

Exercise not only builds up your physical resources, it can also directly combat stress. Many people work off the tensions of the day with a vigorous work out, a run around the park or a dozen laps in the pool.

How does exercise help us cope with stress? One answer may lie in the fact that exercise promotes fitness. It strengthens bodily systems, such as the cardiovascular system, that are affected by stress. Another possibility involves endorphins, the morphine-like hormones that block pain and induce feelings of well-being. Vigorous exercise raises the levels of endorphins in the bloodstream. Exercise also reduces key responses to stress, muscle tension, and anxiety, at least for a few hours.

You need not push your body to extremes to benefit from the stress-reducing effects of exercise. Even mild levels of exercise- a gentle swim, a brisk walk in the park- can relieve stress. Regardless of the reasons that exercise relieves stress, exercise also has a remarkable effect on our moods. It calms us down and improves our psychological outlook. Choose a physical activity that you enjoy. Pushing yourself to do something you detest will only increase the stress you experience.

Change Stressful Thoughts to Stress-Busting Thoughts

What are you telling yourself about the events that distress you? Are you sizing things up correctly, or are you blowing them out of proportion? Do you react to disappointing experiences by feeling disillusioned and hopeless? Do you refuse to compromise? Do you feel miserable when you fall short of your expectations? If these thought patterns ring true, you may wish to replace Black-and-white thoughts with rational alternatives. Allow for shades of grey. Don't focus only on the negative parts of your experiences.

One category of stressful thoughts is thoughts that blow stressors out of proportion. Think of alternative thoughts that help keep things in perspective. For example, a thought that blows stressors out of proportion would be something like: "This is awful. It will never end." A rational alternative thought that would help to keep things in perspective would be: It's bad, but it doesn't have to get the best of me. And upsetting things do come to an end, even if it's sort of hard to believe right now."

Express Your Feelings

When something is bothering you, don't keep it inside. Talk it over with someone you trust. Or write down your feelings in a personal journal. Expressing your feelings is especially helpful in coping with stressful or traumatic events. Keeping disturbing thoughts and feelings to yourself may place additional stress on your autonomic nervous system. The stress can impair your immune system and make you more vulnerable to stress-related disorders. Talking or writing about stressful experiences has positive effects on the immune system.

Try a Little Humour: It's Good Medicine

Humour can help buffer the effects of stress. By making us laugh, humour can get our minds off our troubles, at least for a time. A regular dose of humour may make stress more bearable.

Do Something Each Day That You Enjoy

Stress is more manageable when you do something each day that brings you joy.

Change "I Can't" into "I Can"

A strong sense of self-efficacy[1] enhances our ability to withstand stress. People with higher self-efficacy expectations also bounce back more easily from failure. Life's challenges seem less stressful to them.

If you believe you can accomplish what you set out to do, you are likely to marshal your resources and apply yourself until you reach your goal. If you doubt yourself, you may give up when you encounter the first setback. Start with small achievable goals that will help boost your confidence and encourage you to move forward. Treat disappointments as opportunities to learn from your mistakes.

Practice Relaxing the Mind

Calming the mind induces a relaxed state in which the person's connection with the environment is altered. Worry, planning, and routine concerns are suspended. Consciousness is narrowed to relaxing thoughts. The sympathetic nervous system calms down. The body's alarm reaction is toned down or shut off. This relaxation technique also increases night-time concentrations of the hormone melatonin, which has a relaxing effect and helps people get to sleep.

[1] Self-efficacy is the belief that one can perform a task successfully, and is also the belief in one's abilities.

Moderating Our Stress

Some people are more resilient in the face of stress than others. Though we all have our limits, there is no one-to-one relationship between the amount of stress we experience and outcomes such as physical disorders or psychological distress. Biological factors account for some of the variability in our responses. For example, some people apparently inherit predispositions toward certain physical and psychological disorders. But psychological factors also play a role. Psychological factors can influence, or moderate, the impact of sources of stress.

Our **self-efficacy expectations**[1] affect our ability to withstand stress. Classic research shows that high self-efficacy expectations in the face of stress are associated with lower levels of adrenaline and noradrenaline in the bloodstream. These are hormones that are secreted when we are under stress. They arouse the body in several ways, such as accelerating the heart rate and releasing glucose from the liver. As a result we may have "butterflies in the stomach" and feel nervous. Excessive arousal can impair our ability to manage stress by boosting our motivation beyond optimal levels and by distracting us from the tasks at hand. People with higher self-efficacy expectations thus have biological as well as psychological advantages in managing stress.

People who are self-confident are less prone to be disturbed by adverse events. People with higher self-efficacy expectations are more likely to lose weight or quit smoking and less likely to relapse afterwards. They are also better able to function in spite of pain. Studies have shown that alcohol abuse is correlated with self-efficacy expectations, that is, individuals who believed that they were powerless were more likely to abuse alcohol, perhaps as a way of lessening the stresses in their lives, which may also ring true for drug abuse. People are more likely to try to quit smoking when they believe they can do so successfully. If you think you can, you may well be right.

Psychological hardiness[2] also helps people resist stress. Psychologically hardy people generally have three key characteristics. The characteristics include; commitment, challenge, and control:

Commitment: They tend to involve themselves in, rather than feel alienated from, whatever they do or encounter.

Challenge: They believe that change, rather than stability, is normal in life. They appraise change as an interesting incentive to personal growth, not as a threat to security.

Control: Psychologically hardy people have a high perceived control over their lives. They usually feel and behave as though they are influential, rather than helpless, in facing the various rewards and punishments of life. Psychologically hardy people tend to have what is termed as an internal ***locus of control***[3].

[1] Self-efficacy expectation: The beliefs to the effect that one can perform a task successfully or manage a stressor.

[2] Psychological hardiness: A cluster of traits that buffer stress and are characterized by commitment, challenge, and control. Psychologically hardy individuals are more resilient to the effects of stress. They are committed to their work and other activities, are open to new challenges, and feel in control of their lives.

[3] Locus of control: The perception of control a person has. People who have an *internal* locus of control believe to a great extent that they control their own destiny. Those with an *external* locus of control have the perception that chance or outside forces determine their fate.

Buffering Our Stress

Do you have a sense of humour? Has it ever helped you get through some hard times? The idea that humour lightens the burdens of life and helps people cope with stress has been with us for many centuries. Consider the Biblical maxim: "A merry heart doeth good like a medicine" (proverbs 17:22). It is well known that humour can moderate the effects of stress. In one study carried out on students, it was revealed that students who had a greater sense of humour and produced humour in difficult situations were less affected by negative life events than other students. Yet, we should be cautious, as studies on the effects of humour have yielded inconclusive results.

The ability to <u>predict</u> a stressor can moderate its impact. Question: How do predictability and control help us adjust? Predictability allows us to brace ourselves for the inevitable and, in many cases, plan ways of coping with it. A sense of control is one of the keys to psychological hardiness. Examples from everyday life, including shopping in crowded stores, suggest that a sense of control over the situation - of being able to choose - also helps us cope with the stress of being crammed in. When we are at a concert, disco, or sports event, we may encounter higher intensity than we do in a frustrating ticket line. But, we may be having a wonderful time. Why? Because we have chosen to be at the party, and are focusing on our having a good time. We feel that we are in control. Control - even the illusion of being in control - allows us to feel that we are not at the mercy of the fates. There is also a relationship between the desire to assume control over one's situation and the usefulness of information about impending stressors. Predictability is of greater benefit to people who wish to exercise control over their situations. People who want information about medical procedures and what they will experience, cope better with pain when they undergo those procedures.

Are you the type of person who sees the proverbial glass as half full, or as half empty? People who have optimistic attitudes - who see the glass as half full - tend to be more resilient than others to the effects of stress. One study for example, showed that optimism in pregnant women even predicts better birth outcomes, as measured, for instance, by higher birth weights.

Finally, as well as the psychological concepts mentioned above, sleep seems to help us recover from stress. The amount of sleep we need seems to be genetically determined, but people tend to need more sleep during periods of stress.

Anxiety and Worrying

As we mentioned earlier in the book concerning the definition of anxiety, it is an emotional state that is accompanied by subjective, behavioural, and physical features. Subjective features include worrying, fear of the worst things happening, fear of losing control, nervousness, and inability to relax. Physical features reflect arousal of the sympathetic branch of the autonomic nervous system. They include trembling, sweating, a pounding or racing heart, elevated blood pressure (a flushed face), and faintness. The behavioural features of anxiety are dominated by avoidance of situations or cues associated with the source of the anxiety. For example, dental anxiety is associated with avoidance (or delay) of dental examinations or treatment.

Anxiety is an appropriate response to a real threat. It can be abnormal, however, when it is excessive or when it comes out of nowhere, that is, when events do not seem to warrant it. There are different types of anxiety disorders, but all of them are characterized by excessive or unwarranted anxiety.

According to some surveys, as many as one in five children have psychological difficulties that impair their lives in some way. Anxiety is the most common problem in children under 11, afflicting 10 percent with phobias[1] severe enough to interfere with normal life, another 5 percent with generalized anxiety[2] and constant worry, and another 4 percent with intense anxiety about being separated from their parents.

Worry and anxiety go hand in hand, indeed, worry is almost an exact synonym for anxiety, and vice versa. Worry is the core of anxiety's damaging effect on mental performance of all kinds. Worry, of course, is in one sense a useful response that has gone wayward- an overly zealous mental preparation for an anticipated threat. But such mental rehearsal is a disastrous cognitive impairment when it becomes trapped in a stale routine that captures the entire mind's attention, intruding on all other attempts to focus elsewhere.

Anxiety undermines the intellect. When we worry, or, worry about worrying, then the request to worry about something for a minute can often escalate to contemplation of a lifelong catastrophe: "I'll never be happy." Worries typically follow such lines, a narrative to oneself that jumps from concern and, more often than not, includes catastrophizing, imagining some terrible tragedy. Worries are almost always expressed in the mind's ear, not its eye, that is, in words, not images- a fact that has significance for controlling worry.

Anxiety, researchers observe, comes in two forms: *cognitive* or worrisome thoughts, and *somatic* or the physiological symptoms of anxiety, such as sweating, a racing heart, or muscle tension. In the case of insomnia (the inability to sleep), the main trouble is not somatic arousal, but what keeps people up are intrusive thoughts. Most people with insomnia are chronic worriers and cannot stop worrying, no matter how sleepy they are. The one thing that works in helping such people get to sleep is getting their minds off their worries, focusing instead on the sensations produced by a relaxation method. In short, worries can be stopped by shifting our attention away from them.

Most worriers, however, can't seem to do this. There seems to be a partial pay-off from worrying that highly reinforces the habit. There is, it seems, something 'positive' in worries: worries are ways to deal with potential threats, with dangers that may come one's way. The work of worrying - when it succeeds - is to rehearse what those dangers are, and to reflect on ways to deal with them. But worry doesn't work all that well. New solutions and fresh ways of seeing a problem do not typically come from worrying, especially chronic worry. Instead of coming up with solutions to these potential problems, worriers simply ruminate on the danger itself, immersing themselves in a low-key way in the dread associated with it, while staying in the same pattern of thought.

Chronic worriers worry about a wide range of things, most of which have almost no chance of happening: they read dangers into life's journey that others never notice.

Chronic worriers typically find their worries addictive. Does it really help to run through these same anxious thoughts over and over? Chronic worries come unbidden, that is, we don't invite them, but by their very nature they persist once they arise in the mind. But, one may learn to control the habit of worrying: with self-awareness. With guidance and practice people may learn to identify worries at an earlier point in the anxiety spiral, and learn to monitor cues for anxiety, especially learning to identify situations that trigger worry or the fleeting thoughts and images that initiate the worry, as well as the accompanying sensations of anxiety in the body. Actively creating a relaxed state counters the signals for anxiety that the emotional brain is sending throughout the body.

Anxiety is typically maintained by exaggerating the consequences of threatening events, like meeting new people, or flying, and believing that one is unable to cope with them. Again, one may learn to control this exaggeration and thus better cope with their anxiety.

[1] Phobia is classified as excessive or inappropriate fear of an object or situation.

[2] Generalized Anxiety is a general state of anxiety (not normally attributed to a specific reason) that becomes expressed in the form of persistent worrying.

Anxiety Disorders

In the previous chapter, we mentioned that anxiety is an appropriate response to a real threat but that it is abnormal when it is excessive or when it comes out of nowhere, that is, when events do not seem to warrant it. There are different types of anxiety disorders, but all of them are characterized by excessive or unwarranted anxiety. The anxiety disorder that we shall examine here is Generalized Anxiety Disorder (GAD).

People with Generalized Anxiety Disorder (GAD) seem to worry about every little thing, not just one particular thing. The central feature of GAD is a general state of anxiety that becomes expressed in the form of persistent worrying. The anxiety cannot be attributed to a phobic object, situation, or activity. Rather it seems to have a "free floating" quality.

Other specific anxiety disorders are complicated by panic attacks[1] or other features that are the focus of the anxiety. In GAD, the focus is generalized to the events of everyday life. For a person to be classified with GAD then at least 6 months of excessive anxiety and worry (apprehensive expectation) must be ongoing for more days than not. Furthermore, it must be very difficult to turn off or control the worry process. This is what distinguishes pathological worrying from the normal kind we all experience from time to time as we get ready for an upcoming event or challenge. Most of us worry for a time but can set the problem aside and go on to another task. Even if the upcoming challenge is a big one, as soon as it is over, the worrying stops. For people with GAD it typically never stops, and, they usually turn to the next 'crisis' as soon as the current one is over.

The physical symptoms associated with generalized anxiety are characterized by muscle tension, mental agitation, susceptibility to fatigue (probably the result of long-term excessive muscle tension), some irritability, and difficulty sleeping. Focusing attention is difficult as the mind quickly switches from crisis to crisis.

As we said, people with GAD worry about minor, everyday life events for the most part, a characteristic that distinguishes GAD from other anxiety disorders. When asked, "Do you worry excessively about minor things?" individuals with GAD respond "yes." Of course, major events quickly become the focus of anxiety and worry too. Adults typically focus on possible misfortune to their children, family health, job responsibilities, and more minor things such as household chores or being on time for appointments. Children with GAD most often worry about academic, athletic, or social performance and physical injury.

Most studies find that GAD is associated with an earlier and more gradual beginning than most other anxiety disorders. Many people have felt anxious and tense all their lives. Once it develops, GAD is chronic.

[1] Panic attack is defined as an abrupt experience of intense fear or acute discomfort, accompanied by physical symptoms that usually include heart palpitations, chest pain, shortness of breath, and possibly dizziness.(Read about panic attacks in detail in the chapter Panic Attacks).

Anxiety Disorders II

We saw in the previous chapter that Generalized Anxiety Disorder (GAD) is one type of Anxiety Disorder, and a common one at that.

What causes GAD? Well, as with most anxiety disorders, there may be a genetic contribution. Several studies have shown that Generalized Anxiety Disorder tends to run in families. Specifically, in more recent studies, what seems to be inherited is the tendency to become anxious rather than GAD itself (investigations of anxiety as a human trait show a clear heritable factor).

Interestingly, Individuals with GAD do not respond as strongly as individuals with other anxiety disorders in which panic is most prominent. In fact, several studies have found that individuals with GAD show less responsiveness on most physiological measures, such as heart rate, blood pressure, skin conductance (test that measures sweat levels), and respiration rate, than do individuals with other anxiety disorders.

When individuals with GAD are compared to non-anxious normal people, the one physiological measure that consistently distinguishes them apart is muscle tension. People with GAD are chronically tense. To understand this phenomenon, researchers began to try to discover what goes on in the minds of people with GAD. With new methods from cognitive science, we are beginning to uncover the sometimes *unconscious* mental processes ongoing in GAD.

The evidence indicates that individuals with GAD are highly sensitive to threat in general, particularly to a threat that has personal relevance. That is, they allocate their attention much more readily to sources of threat than people who are not anxious. Furthermore, this acute awareness of potential threat, particularly if it is personal, seems to be entirely automatic or *unconscious*. Findings have shown that people with GAD engage in frantic, intense thought processes or worry without accompanying images.

Typically people with GAD are never able to work through their problems and arrive at solutions. Therefore they become *chronic worriers* with quite severe muscle tension. Intense worrying for an individual with GAD may serve the same maladaptive purpose as avoidance does for people with phobias. It prevents the person from facing the feared situation, and so adaptation never occurs.

In summary, some people inherit a tendency to be tense, and they develop a sense early on that important events in their lives may be uncontrollable and potentially dangerous. Significant stress makes them apprehensive and vigilant. This sets off intense worry with resulting physiological changes, leading to generalized anxiety disorder. This is consistent with our definition of anxiety as a future-oriented mood state focused on potential danger or threat, as opposed to an emergency or alarm reaction to actual present danger. As well as other treatments, helping people with this disorder to focus on what is actually threatening is helpful.

Panic Attacks

The roots of panic experience are deeply embedded in our cultural myths. Pan, the Greek god of nature, lived in the country, presiding over rivers, woods, streams, and grazing animals. But Pan did not look like the typical god. He was very ugly and short, with legs resembling a goat's. Unfortunately for travellers, Pan often took a nap in a small cave or bush near the road. When travelling Greeks disturbed him, he let out a blood-curdling scream that was so intense, many terrified travellers died of fright. This sudden overwhelming reaction came to be known as **panic**, after the irate god. In psychology, a **panic attack** is defined as an abrupt experience of intense fear or acute discomfort, accompanied by physical symptoms that usually include heart palpitations, chest pain, shortness of breath, and, possibly, dizziness.

There are basically three types of panic attacks: situationally bound, unexpected, and situationally predisposed. If you know you are afraid of high places or of driving in the mountains, you might have a panic attack in these situations but not anywhere else; this is a *situationally bound* (cued) panic attack. By contrast, you might experience *unexpected* (uncued) panic attacks. The third type of panic attack, the *situationally predisposed*, is in between. You are more likely, but not inevitably, to have an attack where you have had one before, for example, in a large shopping centre. If you don't know whether it will happen today, and it does, the attack is situationally predisposed.

In **panic disorder**, people experience abrupt attacks of acute, intense anxiety or sheer terror. At first these attacks <u>are not</u> triggered by a specific object or situation. They seem to come "out of the blue." But over time they may come to be associated with cues[1] in situations in which they have occurred, such as boarding an elevator or aeroplane. People with panic disorder have strong physical symptoms such as shortness of breath, heavy sweating, tremors, and pounding of the heart. It is not unusual for them to think they are having a heart attack. Many panic sufferers have difficulty breathing and may feel as though they are suffocating. They may also experience nausea, numbness or tingling, flushes, or chills, and fear of going crazy or losing control. Panic attacks may last minutes or hours. Afterwards, the person usually feels drained.

Because people with panic disorder never know when a panic attack might occur, they develop what is called **agoraphobia;** a fear and avoidance of situations in which they would feel unsafe in the event of a panic attack or symptoms of it. These situations include those from which it would be hard or embarrassing to get help or escape to one's home or to a hospital. In severe cases, people with this type of disorder are totally unable to leave the house, sometimes for years on end.

We should mention here that many people who have panic attacks do not necessarily develop panic disorder. Similarly, many people experience anxiety and panic without developing agoraphobia.

To meet the criteria for panic disorder (with or without agoraphobia) a person must experience an unexpected panic attack and develop substantial anxiety over the possibility of having another attack or about the implications of the attack or its consequences. In other words, he or she must think that each attack is a sign of impending death or incapacitation. A few individuals do not report concern about another attack but still change their behaviour in a way that indicates the distress the attacks cause them. They may avoid going to certain places or neglect their duties around the house for fear an attack might occur if they are too active.

An individual who has not had a panic attack for years may still have strong agoraphobic avoidance. Agoraphobic avoidance seems to be determined by the extent to which you think or expect you might have another attack rather than by how many attacks you actually have or how severe they are. Thus agoraphobic avoidance is simply one way of coping with unexpected panic attacks.

Other methods of coping with panic attacks include using (and eventually abusing) drugs and/or alcohol. Some individuals do not actually avoid agoraphobic situations but endure them with "intense dread." For example, people who simply must go to work each day or, perhaps, travel as part of the job will suffer untold agonies of anxiety and panic, simply to achieve their goals. Thus, agoraphobia mat be characterized either by avoiding the situations or by enduring them with marked distress.

Panic disorder with or without agoraphobia is fairly common. Approximately 3.5% of the population meets the criteria for panic disorder at some point during their lives, two thirds of them are women.

[1] A cue, in psychological terms, can be anything (a place, a smell, a face, a feeling, etc.) that provokes a similar response within an individual as something we are already familiar with. For example, if you were in some place and you smelt this particularly wonderful fragrance, then when you smell that fragrance again, even after a long time, it is highly likely, you will bring to memory the place where you smelt it the first time. Hence, the fragrance serves as a **cue** for remembering the place.

Post Traumatic Stress

So terrible has been the experience of many combat veterans, accident and disaster survivors, and sexual assault victims, including an estimated two thirds of prostitutes. Stretch a metal spring and it will snap back- unless stretched too far. Traumatic stress - experiencing or witnessing severely threatening, uncontrollable events with a sense of fear, helplessness, or horror - can produce *post-traumatic stress disorder*, symptoms of which include haunting memories and nightmares, a numbed social withdrawal, jumpy anxiety, and insomnia.

The emotional disorder that follows a trauma is known as **post-traumatic stress disorder (PTSD)**. In psychology, the setting event for PTSD is exposure to a traumatic event during which a person feels fear, helplessness, or horror. Afterwards, victims re-experience the event through memories and nightmares. PTSD may not begin for many months or years after exposure to trauma, but it may last for years or even decades afterwards. When memories occur very suddenly and the victims find themselves reliving the event, they are having a *flashback*. Victims avoid anything that reminds them of the trauma. They display a characteristic restriction or numbing of emotional responsiveness, which may be very disruptive to interpersonal relationships. They are sometimes unable to remember certain aspects of the event. Victims may unconsciously attempt to avoid the experience of emotion itself, like people with panic disorder (mentioned in the previous chapter), because intense emotions could bring back memories of the trauma. Finally, victims typically are chronically over-aroused, easily startled, and quick to anger.

PTSD is subdivided into *acute* and *chronic*. Acute PTSD can be diagnosed between 1 and 3 months after the event occurs. When PTSD continues longer than 3 months, it is considered chronic. Chronic PTSD is usually associated with more prominent avoidance behaviours, as well as with the more frequent co-occurrence of additional disorders such as social phobia. In the delayed onset of PTSD, individuals show few if any symptoms immediately after a trauma, but later, perhaps years afterwards, they develop full-blown PTSD.

As we already mentioned, PTSD cannot be diagnosed until roughly a month after the trauma. A new disorder in psychopathology is **acute stress disorder**. This is really PTSD occurring within the first month after the trauma, but the different name emphasizes the very severe reaction that some people have immediately. In acute stress disorder, PTSD-like symptoms are accompanied by other symptoms, such as amnesia for all or part of the trauma, emotional numbing, or feelings of unreality. In many cases, acute stress disorder leads to the development of PTSD. We should note that combat and sexual assault are the most common traumas.

At lower levels of trauma, some people develop PTSD but most do not. What accounts for these differences? As with other disorders, we bring our own generalized biological and psychological vulnerabilities with us. The greater the vulnerability, the more likely we are to develop PTSD. If certain characteristics run in your family, you have a much greater chance of developing the disorder. A family history of anxiety suggests a generalized biological vulnerability for PTSD

Also, there seems to be a generalized psychological vulnerability described in the context of other disorders based on early experiences with unpredictable or uncontrollable events. Studies have shown that at high levels of trauma, these vulnerabilities do not matter much. However, at low levels of stress or trauma, vulnerabilities matter a great deal in determining whether the disorder will develop. Family instability is one factor that may instil a sense the world is an uncontrollable, potentially dangerous place, so it is not surprising that individuals from unstable families are at risk for developing PTSD if they experience trauma.

To demonstrate this point further, a study was carried out in 1997 on two different groups of torture victims. Thirty-four survivors had no history of political activity, commitment to a political cause or group, or expectations of arrest and torture. Compared with 55 tortured political activists, the non-activists were subjected to less horrendous abuse but showed higher levels of psychopathology. It seemed that the political activists were more prepared psychologically for torture, which they generally experienced as predictable, thereby reducing later psychological symptoms. This study further demonstrates psychological factors that either protect against or increase the risk of developing PTSD.

As this is the last chapter in the book, I would like to remind you that we may be better able to protect our health during times of stress simply by writing about the sources of stress in our lives. Evidence suggests that writing about stressful events may reduce physical symptoms and improve immune system functioning. There may be benefits to the time-honoured custom of keeping a diary of your daily experiences, stresses and all. Even if writing about the stresses in your life doesn't improve your physical health, it may help relieve the psychological effects of daily stress.

# Afterword

As we mentioned in the beginning of this book, stress is inevitable. We always try to reduce and eliminate stress in different ways. When the ways and means we use do not bring the desired results, we struggle, and become tired, often exhausted. Some of us accept that life and stress are part and parcel, and get by as best we can. Others try to *escape* from it by using drugs, alcohol and other harmful ways, while others choose healthier ways by listening to music, going to movies, shopping, exercise and other hobbies, which help them distract themselves from the 'stressors' which are taxing them, and try to relax.

The main key though, is to strike at the core of the issues causing us stress. The above serve only to temporarily alleviate the uncomfortable *symptoms* of stress. Our cognition is, if not everything, then almost everything, in dealing with what is stressing us. By talking with friends, coaching ourselves, speaking with a grandparent or other member of the family, or speaking with a counsellor, we can maybe find a new way of looking at things, of interpreting them – being flexible in our thinking to adjust our reaction to the current stressor is an important step in reducing the *effect* of the stressor. 'Cognitive reframing', that is, adjusting our thought patterns and processes, is a great weapon to have in our arsenal to buffer and mediate the *impact* of stress on us.

I hope you enjoyed this book.

The Psychology and Health series

Stress: We Can Master It.

Depression and Sadness: Never Lose Hope – Even If You Can't See Any.

Drugs and Addictions: Some Things You Might Know, A lot of Things You Might Not.

Body Image: How We See Ourselves and Others; How This Can Lead to Problems.

Know Thyself: The Eternal Struggle of The Heart and Mind.

I Want to Sleep: Why We Struggle to Sleep – How We Can Remedy It.

www.ingramcontent.com/pod-product-compliance
Lightning Source LLC
Chambersburg PA
CBHW070229290526
45789CB00004B/1545